Other books by Philip Salisbury

The Current Economic Crisis and the Great Depression
Xlibris

Economic Crisis: Explanation and Policy Options
University Press of America

I'm FED UP with the Tea Party!
Infinity Press

A Time That Was: Experiences of a Peace Corps Volunteer in Liberia, West Africa, 1962–1964

LIFE AS PROCESS

PHILIP S. SALISBURY

authorHOUSE®

AuthorHouse™
1663 Liberty Drive
Bloomington, IN 47403
www.authorhouse.com
Phone: 1 (800) 839-8640

Published by AuthorHouse 02/05/2018

ISBN: 978-1-5462-1786-2 (sc)
ISBN: 978-1-5462-1784-8 (hc)
ISBN: 978-1-5462-1785-5 (e)

Library of Congress Control Number: 2017917673

Print information available on the last page.

CONTENTS

INTRODUCTION

This essay is about observation and process. It addresses what we observe, how we observe, and the value and consequences of how we observe. It also explores the terms of value and meaning, the attribution of value and meaning to observation, and the process of existence.

Second, this essay examines time and change and how we observe both. It discusses the concept of "living in the now" or "living in the moment" and examines its relevance to a life well-lived.

Third, it proposes a framework for observing

reality. The framework suggests not only that we can observe life from a global perspective but that we have the capacity to experience reality at multiple levels. This is where the empiricist confronts the level-of-analysis issue.

Fourth, the essay explores our human and assisted levels of observation. This represents a broad spectrum of innate as well as chemical, physical, and electronic devices that allow us to explore our universe, our relationships, and our personal lives.

Fifth, the text investigates various methods that humans have employed to rationalize their understandings of reality. Included in the discussion is the relevance of these practices to an individual's personal life.

In addition, the essay discusses observing the world as it is and the difficulties inherent in maintaining objectivity while observing precisely.

One of the conditions of our current environment is

the loss of pragmatism. Ideologies are now dominant in our political discourse, be it local, statewide, national, or international. In such an environment, compromise becomes unlikely. There is a black and a white with no room for gray. The essay discusses the eventual, and alternative, consequences of this.

A. P. French wrote a book in 1971 titled *Vibrations and Waves*. On reading the book, I became impressed by the diversity in physics of wave forms and their ubiquitous nature. It was not until I was doing some social research at my job that the process of the generation and decline of waves and wave patterns became personally relevant to me.

A wave does not exist by itself. It exists in an environment with other waves. The varieties of waves interact, creating the growth and decline of the wave forms. There also could be created different patterns of a wave form.

Physics has developed a set of diverse equations to characterize waves in their simple and more complex forms. In addition, a range of instruments have been developed that make it possible to visualize, analyze, and monitor many forms of waves.

It all starts with the continuum of existence, which can be characterized in the following words:

<>declining<>----<>maintaining<>----<>growing<>

The arrowheads (> <) denote the process of transition from one status to another. At the extremes of the continuum (< on the left and > on the right), change into another form occurs. Furthermore, at the extremes of the continuum, > on the left and < on the right mean return from partial decline or growth.

All existence fits into this simple framework, some things in more complex ways than others.

The diversity in existence is so extensive that it is beyond any one mind's comprehension. There exists a range of approaches to studying this existence. Some physicists study existence at the subatomic level, while others study it at the atomic level. There are molecular physicists and biologists. It is possible to go from the subatomic to the larger study of plants, animals, populations, planets, moons, stars, black holes, and all of space.

It is my hope that this book will raise questions and new observations on your part about your own worldview. It is important that you approach this essay with an open and inquiring mind. Not everyone will agree, but hopefully important questions will be raised and some discussion will take place. Let's begin.

CHAPTER 1

THE PRESENT MOMENT OR THE NOW

Individuals who write about the present moment emphasize that nothing ever happens in the future or the past; it happens in the now. Sometimes this is demonstrated by a click of the fingers to establish being present in the moment. I am moved to ask, *What if you click your fingers a second time?* The first click, which can only be remembered or recorded in some way, is in the past. Thus, the moment is juxtaposed with the past. Our experience is of the continuity of past, present, and future.

However, once our experience of the now has passed, we can never recall it in the same form with all its nature, texture, color, nuance, beauty, or plainness. As humans, we have the capacity to remember the emotional past in the form of memories we store in our nervous systems, in our musculature, or in our bodily tissues (such as the fascia). We can recall images or memories of past events either consciously or unconsciously.

Alternatives may present themselves in which we get to experience the results of passing moments from years, millennia, or light-years into the past. Recalling personal memories, examining the rings of the cross-section of a tree, observing the depths and layers of sandstone in the Grand Canyon, and viewing the signals and photos obtained from distant galaxies using the Hubble telescope are all observations we do in the now to observe history in its various forms. What is important about our ability to do this? For sure, it makes life more interesting. The variety of experiences that can be explored is extensive. For some, it is a source of awe and curiosity.

There is one overarching truth about experiencing the future, the now, and the past. *Life is process.* In fact, *existence is process.* The process consists of future becoming present, the present becoming past. This process is pervasive.

So what can be surmised? Why is this process so pervasive? The presence of process means that change is occurring in a myriad of ways. We now have understood a central fact of existence. Change is occurring in a variety of ways, paces, and rates. It may be at a daily or seasonal pace, and it occurs at different types of time intervals, from nanoseconds to light-years. Farmers are astute observers of change. Millions of wage or salaried workers commute to and from work in regular, twice-daily intervals. Seasonally, road workers prepare their equipment and clean up snow, and as the season passes, they tear the equipment down.

The moon goes through its regular and predictable cycle, from showing a sliver of visibility to becoming full. The sun rises daily, providing different hours of daylight to different parts of the globe. A habitual pattern of mealtimes is, for some, three per day. Sleep time, for most, is relegated to naps and the nighttime hours.

We expect some type of regularity with many of life's experiences. Such occurrences become so regular that we approach them almost unnoticed and with a minimum of observation.

CHAPTER 2

CHANGE AND TIME

Chapter 1 introduced us to life as process and the process of change. The two are inseparable. Imagine if everything in the world were immobile—from the quarks in an electron to the rotation of the earth on its axis and in its orbit around the sun. No one would be out walking, bicycling, driving cars, riding trains, or taking airplanes. Knowing what we do and having experienced what we have, this is an unimaginable scenario.

A child originates as the combination of an ovum and a sperm. The fetus grows in the womb, and when the child is born, the infant grows into a preschooler, a grade-schooler, a junior high student, an adolescent in high school, and then possibly a college graduate who furthers his or her development as a young adult. Barring illnesses or accidents, the young adult matures and continues to an age when his or her physical prowess declines. The process of aging sets in. Retirement may be a possibility. Aging into retirement, physical changes take place. These physical changes of aging accompany the individual to eventual decline and death. Where in this scenario, and in the environment surrounding it, are there not changes? The most accurate response is that change is always taking place.

Time is a way in which we measure such change. If there is no change, there is no time or manner in which to determine time. Time is a way of capturing change for pragmatic purposes. If you consider all the manners of determining time that exist, all rely on change taking place. The type of change, particularly with clocks and watches, is a change in position. Can you recall any type of time-telling that does not feature some form of change?

Early humans did not have timepieces. They were unaware of seconds, minutes, and hours. They awoke by the rhythms of the natural world. Sunrise and sunlight allowed them to conduct the activities essential to their lives. They hunted, fished, and gathered food and made their tools and shelters. They understood what animals would be doing at specific times, in addition to the seasonality of fruits; in fact, people used to live according to their circadian rhythms.

Some animals live in underground caves or deep in the ocean. They have body rhythms that allow them to survive in an environment where there is no day or night. These body rhythms allow them to eat, sleep, awake, and reproduce in regular patterns. Other natural forms of time and rhythm are evident in the tides caused by the moon, in plant behavior, in the nocturnal behavior of some animals and birds, in the movement of plankton in the ocean, and in the variation in hours of sunlight at the earth's poles.

Approximately five hundred years ago, humans discovered that the seasons they experienced were caused by the manner in which the earth tilted on its axis. At approximately the same time, Copernicus came to understand that the sun was the center of our solar system. The Chinese year was measured by the sun, with months calculated by the moon's movements. The Julian calendar remedied the problem of having extra days by having seven months with thirty-one days, four with thirty days, and one with twenty-eight days. Every four years, an extra day was added because a solar year does not add up exactly to three hundred sixty-five days. Those years have been labeled leap years. But nature does not care about its calendar.

In fact, the solar year is shorter than three hundred sixty-five and one-quarter days. More exactly, the annual calendar year is eleven minutes and fourteen seconds shorter than the standard three hundred sixty-five and one-quarter days. Taking this into account, the Gregorian calendar was formed. We use this calendar today.

Most adults in a postindustrial society accept having a regular calendar and watches to keep track of daily time. We make appointments, have designated times to go to and leave work, and count up our vacation and sick time in time units. But how is time experienced?

I propose that time be experienced not in the momentary now but as a process of moments, as continuity. For any physical object, these moments are blended into a process known as "duration." To repeat, the present is the future becoming past. This process of moments has been termed "flow" by Csikszentmihalyi (1990) or as "becoming" by me. The future is becoming the present is becoming the past. This is not the *now,* as some would maintain. It is the *process of becoming.*

Life is a composite of wave forms. There is the process of being born, the process of existing, the process of decline and death. In shorthand:

future > present > past

That is the linear view of existence. The future is becoming, the present is becoming, and the past is becoming. In a curvilinear view of existence, the past may become the present, or the past may become the future. An alternative view is that the three words represent life as process.

CHAPTER 3

DURATION AND TRANSITIONS

Webster's New Universal Unabridged Dictionary defines *duration* as "the length of time something continues or exists." In effect, duration is another way of defining time. Every object or waveform that exists currently has duration. To observe duration, it is sometimes possible to observe the characteristics of an object or waveform at its time of origin and continue that observation until the moment of the object or waveform's extinction. Duration thus equals the time from the origin of something to its defined extinction.

What are some examples of this? The signs of a baby's gestation are evident from about the first trimester on. However, it is difficult, if not impossible, to observe this process continuously at every moment, as one has to sleep, wake, work, eat, and play. Another example is the duration of the fall season in Vermont. Each day may bring a different panorama of colors outside one's kitchen window. However, it is difficult to be in the moment continuously with joy over the intensity and variety of colors that present themselves. One has to break the moment with routine chores of life and survival. This does not inhibit appreciation of the beauty of the leaves, but it does make continuous existence in the moment unlikely. However, existence remains continuous. It is becoming.

Durations have a special quality. They are patterns assumed by living and inanimate things. Duration has an assigned starting time (usually normatively established) and transitions to its time of extinction. This means there are changes in the characteristics of the beginning animate or inanimate object. These changes may be predictable or unpredictable. The larger implication of this is that either the moment had to be a big one, or there had to be a string of moments from origination to extinction during which the animate or inanimate object existed. I believe a continuity exists that can be called an object's history. The durations of objects are continual; that string of moments and overlapping of the durations of objects is a continuity.

The history of someone or an object is this compilation of moments, its duration. The recording of these moments may or may not take place. The recording of each moment is usually unlike each moment itself. For individuals, moments become aggregated into experience. This experience may be stored as mental memories gathered by the senses, muscle memories, or fascia memories. Experiencing the now means that we experience change. The now consists of moment after moment being "chained" together into what we term *experience or continuity.*

There are two types of continuity: the continuity of *cohorts* and the continuity of *overlapping cohorts.*

Many of the changes we are exposed to as humans may be categorized as transitions. Such changes, or transitions, do much either in response to interests we have in life or make life interesting. Many are unexpected, unplanned for, and some may even be inevitable. Importantly, changes provide for life and its many transitions. Life would not be of interest or possible without them.

Continua and Reality

All reality, including space, is in process. All reality consists of continua. The continuum at the basis of reality is

<>antimatter----<>matter<>----<>energy<>

Continua are a conceptual way of describing different aspects of our diverse physical, biological, social, economic, and behavioral worlds. Another way of conceptualizing all continua is as follows:

<>diminishing<>----<>maintaining<>----<>growing<>

This continuum purposely uses gerunds that indicate an ongoing process. Also, at the terminal stages of the continuum are arrowheads pointing beyond the concepts of diminishing and growing. Why? This is so because diminishing can continue to the point of diffusion or extinction. This is also true of the concept of growing. Growing can continue to the time of diffusion or extinction. This represents a definitional issue for the observer.

As components and aggregates of reality are observed in their general and specific forms, several descriptive truths will become evident. These truths fit into a systematic theoretical perspective useful in understanding many different types of phenomena. The focus of this treatise will be on humans, their components, their context, and the relationships they are part of, participate in, and create. In these matters of focus, there is a general, relative continuum that can be characterized in the following way:

<>deficit----<>equilibrium<>----<>surplus<>

Application of this general continuum, in specific and diverse ways, will be a major focus of this book.

Continua and the Concept of Limits

Earlier, a generalized continuum, <>deficit<> equilibrium<>surplus<>, was presented. A continuum exists for each defined component and its characteristics. It varies from the component's level at the time of origination to its level at the time of depletion. For the characteristics (x) of the components of any given aggregate, there may be a continuum used to describe the characteristics. A component may have multiple characteristics that are described by identifying the appropriate continua. The extremes of the continua represent characteristics or values at which the continua become nonexistent or transformed. There are two ways of describing transitions that may occur. Any change in the number of units participating in a component is, by definition, a decrease in the number of units in the component. Second, changes in the characteristics of any of the units that make up a component result in a decrease in the number of units in the component or a change in the component. This makes clear why it is necessary to include in a component only those units that have the characteristics that are part of the component and affect the duration of the component. The observer may, by choice, include *secondary characteristics* that have no effect on the duration of the component. This is unnecessary. Several examples of continua are as follows:

0<>----<>heart beats per minute<>----<>maximum<>

<>minimum<>----<>stress levels<>----<>maximum<>

<>minimum<>----<>functional brain cells<>----<>maximum<>

0<>----<>number of positive stimulations<>maximum<>

0<>----<>rate of physical child abuse<>----<>maximum<>

0<>----<>number of books read per month<>----<>maximum<>

0<>----<>hours of TV watched per week<>----<>maximum<>

<>minimum<>----<>achievement level<>maximum

<>laissez-faire<>----<>balanced

parenting<>----<>authoritarian<>

<>minimum<>----<>ratio of dependents to

earning population<>----<>maximum<>

<>minimum<>monthly disposable income<>maximum<>

0<>----<>family income level<>----<>maximum<>

<>minimum<>----<>annual profit (or loss)----<>maximum<>

<>minimum<>----<>state budget<>----<>maximum<>

<>minimum<>----<>federal budget deficit<>----<>maximum<>

All continua exist within limits, just as there are limits to the minimum and maximum speed of any physical object within a defined frame of reference. The nature of the limits may be affected by one or more factors external to a given continuum as well as by factors that are internal to it. The continuum exists for all of the units and characteristics of the component. When the characteristic varies outside the value of the characteristic, the unit is no longer part of the component. Similarly, when the number of units of a component decreases to 0 or becomes nonexistent, it is no longer part of an aggregate.

This presentation is concerned with a general theory that applies to all aspects of human development and their interaction with surrounding environments that can have personal, family, community, or societal consequences. The theoretical framework is applied to humans, human organization, and human environments, despite its more general applicability.

One situation violates this demographic concept of cohorts' coming into existence and declining until death (or change). That exception is the Higgs boson. At the CERN Particle Accelerator in Switzerland, two streams of protons were accelerated in opposite directions, and then they collided. Observations were made of the colliding particles. As the particles declined in energy, there was a point along the declining curve line at which the line displayed a point (p) at which $p_2 > p_1$. This increase was interpreted as energy being released as the protons decelerated.

CHAPTER 4

AGGREGATES AND COMPONENTS

The scientific world of the physicist has been marked by the gradual discovery of smaller and smaller particles ending with hypothetical particles termed quarks, which are believed to constitute all particles, termed baryons or mesons. In our everyday experience, however, the definitions of smaller and smaller subatomic particles are not recognized. Most observers do not appreciate the relevance of this knowledge to understanding the nature of our universe. While these discoveries have been made, there is growing knowledge that assists humans in understanding the nature of the world we live in from the global to the subatomic level. This approach addresses what is known as the "level of analysis issue" in the social sciences.

Let's assume you are an environmentally conscious individual who wishes to work cooperatively with a group of citizens toward getting smoking-ban legislation passed for all public places, including retail establishments. Several significant questions must be initially addressed. Is the legislative change targeting city, county, or state-wide legislative and executive governing bodies? The decision as to which level of governance to approach will impact the type of existing organizational framework and the resources required for the effort. The following diagram demonstrates the basic framework that is presented for this decision.

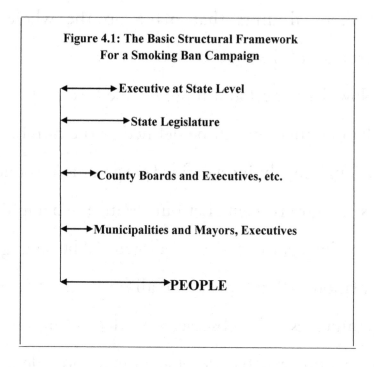

Figure 4.1: The Basic Structural Framework
For a Smoking Ban Campaign

Executive at State Level

State Legislature

County Boards and Executives, etc.

Municipalities and Mayors, Executives

PEOPLE

This schematic is a basic hierarchical abstract diagram representing an overview of some of the components of a system campaign for a smoking ban.

Some units, such as townships, water districts, electrical districts, and so on, have been omitted. What is the principle in operation here? The state is, for some purposes, an aggregate. It contains diverse levels and forms of governance. These are component governmental units that make up the whole of governance of the state.

Now, let's develop a more detailed example. The civilian population can be defined as the number of individuals inhabiting a defined geographic area under the same government. Let our defined geographical area be the continental United States. The aggregate population includes people of all sexes, all ages, and all ethnicities. The observer can, depending on the information available, develop a much more detailed view of the population. One can divide the population into a set of mutually exclusive groups or *components.* How can these components be defined? One way to define the components would be to first select all component states making up the continental United States. A second set of *subcomponents* would be those of sex, age, and education level. The important principle is that each division into components and subcomponents be mutually exclusive.

If, for example, one takes the population of the continental United States and disaggregates it in the previously mentioned fashion, a much clearer definition is obtained. We would know where the population is located, its sex and age distribution, and ultimately how educated the US population is in different states and for different sex and age subcomponents.

Why do this? Because it lends detail to an otherwise blurry picture. Why do we focus the lens of a camera before taking a picture? To assure that the picture is as highly defined as possible. In addition, the understanding of aggregates and components presented allows us in some small ways to begin to understand some systems with fairly well-defined patterns of variation.

In our interpersonal interactions, we do not interact with and observe individuals as their various parts all the time. First, there are boundary issues. For example, where do the lips end and the skin begin?

Where do the other person's spatial boundaries end and mine begin? Second, the focus of our attention on an individual with whom we are in conversation may be affected by how far away we are from that person. The closer we are, the more of the individual's head and torso we see. The farther away we are, the more of an individual's full profile we see. Our sense of the individual may include important emotions of friendship, love, dislike, or stronger negative emotions in addition to the visual images we observe.

Thus, when we make observations of another human, we have a choice about what observations to make. What part(s) of the human dress or anatomy do we focus on? Or in general, we may choose to focus on all the parts (i.e., the big picture within our field of vision). Importantly, there is also how long we choose to focus our attention on a particular scene. It is the process of focusing that has been at the heart of yoga, tai chi, martial arts, prayer, exercise, and other practices such as meditation.

This book has several purposes. At a general level, it is meant to provide a bridge between macro and micro understandings of our diverse physical, biological, social, economic, and behavioral worlds. It provides a theoretical foundation to be used in diverse areas of inquiry. And the algorithms presented herein have an applied value. This may take the form of direct use of the mathematical and probabilistic statements presented herein or a more general application of the concepts to better understand observed phenomena.

These ideas have to confront several issues if they are to remain valid. Theory of the type presented here must be valid at a macro as well as a micro level. The encompassing and sound nature of theory is what makes it both explicative and useful. Any valid theory must be basic enough that it cannot be revised using one or more particular observations. In such a situation, the units of analysis become paramount. What the observer finds on a consistent basis is that there is complexity of many different forms and units. Identifying the source and nature of the complexity results in the possibility of better understanding the phenomena being observed. Social theory needs to start at a basic enough level to be explanatory or even accurately descriptive.

It is important to recognize that the phenomena we observe cannot be equated with the actual observations themselves. Observations consist of interactions with the phenomena being observed. Observations are not the phenomena themselves. Observation may affect the results of the observation (see the *Heisenberg uncertainty principle* and the *Hawthorne Effect*). This is a basic tenet of scientific observation. Our images and even mathematical portrayals are descriptive and predictive in nature. The development of excellent predictive models is based on accurate observation and generalization. The lack of a conceptual framework for observation may result in both observational and predictive errors that seriously curtail our understanding of social phenomena.

Ultimate Causes and Reductionism

Alexander's (1987) discussion of proximate causes and reductionism in evolutionary biology raises some issues relative to this theoretical presentation. One form of biological "reductionism" refers to the reduction of explanations to proximate mechanisms (near-term causes or physically identifiable components). In its extreme form, this type of reductionism questions, "Is a trait, variation, or behavior genetically determined?" There is the importance of remaining aware that unjustified assumptions about determinism or preprogramming can be made. Alexander focuses on the form of biological reductionism that he terms "the development of general evolutionary principles … usually referred to as the search for *ultimate causes.*" He maintains that establishing principles is reduction or simplification. It is not a reductionism that primarily seeks partial or proximate causes. The approach seeks generalizations explaining phenomena that, in the absence of such generalizations, appear more complex as well as (sometimes) more mysterious.

The reduction of phenomena by dissection sometimes improves our understanding of the phenomena. Such dissection requires the identification and definition of smaller and smaller units. Reduction by generalization requires the development of new approaches to observation and new ideas.

It is my view that connections between the aggregate level and the component level of observation, as well as between aggregate and aggregate, need to be made for successful behavioral, social welfare, and environmental policy to be developed and implemented. The component and aggregate units of analysis are *related* to individuals, families, groups, businesses, organizations, communities, cities, counties, states, nations, environments, economies, and the materials and systems they are part of and create. Second, the observations are related to aspects of being, expression, behavior, and interaction for the units of analysis under consideration.

Aggregate time-series observations may include component observations. In aggregate analysis of a common unit of analysis (say, population), further subgroupings of the unit of aggregate analysis can be made (e.g., sex, age, race, geographical location, IQ, socioeconomic status, etc.). The subgroupings at a given time (t) add to the total of the aggregate at time t. These subgroupings are the interactive components of the aggregate. The aggregate, while used often in analysis and for generalization, always has its component parts, which, in effect, create the aggregate and influence the behavior of the aggregate. The components are in turn influenced by the behavior of the aggregate and its subgroupings.

Categories of Change Processes

When aggregates are decomposed into subgroupings, if the subgrouping is clearly defined as a component, the components have some generalized patterns of development, origination, and decline that are graphically characterized in the following diagram.

The five categories of change processes, development, maintenance, decline, and change of position, are basic and universal. *Developing* can mean originating, increasing, or developing. Maintaining can occur by retention of the status quo or maintenance by replacement or exchange. *Declining* means decreasing or changing of form. Change of position is a change in the spatial coordinates of a unit, object, or a form of antimatter, matter, or energy.

The Universe of Matter and Energy as Aggregate and Particulate

All matter is particulate. Matter has been discovered to consist of atomic particles and subatomic particles. It is known that energy and matter are directly related ($E = mc^2$). There are numerous physical as well as ecological perspectives on the nature of matter and energy. The first law of thermodynamics is that of the conservation of energy, stating that mechanical energy can be changed into heat energy at a defined rate. The second law of thermodynamics states that heat cannot pass from a cold body to a warm body. Later, Planck developed quantum theory in his efforts to explain radiant energy. He found that radiation is not a continuous process but that energy is emitted in small packets of various sizes, always containing an integral multiple of units called *quanta*. Matter and energy are thus, at their physical and energetic base, particulate in nature. Particle theory is constantly evolving and continues to depend on the construction of different forms of particle acceleration and management equipment as well as changing theory. With the evolution of particle theory, the laws of conservation continue to be found to be true.

These physical perspectives have applicability to humans and related systems. First, it is important to understand that all human reality is "particulate" at its base. *Particulate* means that it appears in some unitary form or, if aggregate, a blend of unitary forms. These units may exist at one time, exist over time, cease to exist, or change. From a theoretical and applied perspective, the major analytical decisions to be made are what categories and units are observed, how they will be observed, and whether the observation process affects the phenomena.

What relevance does this "particulate" nature of reality have on the temporal, spatial, physical, biological, behavioral, social, economic, political, and environmental phenomena that constitute our human existence? One example is that of a recently constructed house. From one perspective, the house can be defined as "one" house. A second perspective is to detail its location or coordinates, while a third perspective is to declare its purchase price. A fourth perspective is to declare its current market value, a fifth perspective is to describe its square footage, and a sixth perspective is to describe the ratio of glass to wall space. Still a seventh perspective is to describe the number of rooms and baths in the house. Numerous other perspectives can be used to describe the house (the number of bedrooms, its exterior color, type of roof, garage type, etc.). It is clear that the detailing of observations about this one home could progress for some time before all possibilities are exhausted. A contractor would look at the home in terms of the cost of time and materials it took to build the home and his expected and real profit. An owner would be more concerned with the expenses of the house, the functional and aesthetic qualities of the home, its location, and other factors. That the contractor and the homeowner have different perspectives is important. The contractor is concerned with every two-by-four, door, piece of particleboard, shingle, fixture, furnishing, and cabinet used in the construction of the house as well as the labor (hours) and money (dollars and cents) invested in its construction. This truly reveals the particulate nature of the house as well as the contractor's concerns. The owner of the house has a specifically different set of "particulate" preferences and concerns. When aggregated, the materials and the concerns result in something called a "house." Similarly, from an owner's perspective, it becomes important because of the combination of particulate characteristics that the house has. The number of bedrooms, floor space, carpeting, furnishings, location, floor plan, and even the "feel" of the house are particulate in nature.

From the perspective of human perception, the particulate nature of reality becomes blurred. There is an illusion of wholeness. We do not see a light wave as a composite of photons (which it is). We do not see a house, as we live in it, as a combination of doors, windows, appliances, electrical wiring, paint, boards, and so on. It is unnecessary for us to do so from a functional perspective. Nonetheless, an underlying, particulate reality is there. It understands the particulate reality relevant to human growth and development, human behavior, and the behavior of systems they are part of that is essential to the formulation of effective policies at an individual and a macro level. The connections are present. It is important to recognize this in any theoretical perspective developed for any discipline of thought.

A similar case can be made for the composition and

functioning of the human being. Human particulate nature is undeniable. The structure of amino acids and chemicals that constitute our cells, organs, systems and bodies are examples of how particulate reality is organized into components and aggregates, depending on the frame of reference. From the perspective of those who study humans, the diversity of perspectives is far-ranging. A molecular geneticist is trying to define the structure of a small segment of the human genome, while a political scientist is involved in the study of the impact of sound bites or language on public voting patterns. A cell biologist is trying to assess the chemical functioning of mitochondria, while a population theorist is interested in defining multivariate explanations of rates of conception that rely on diverse economic, quality of life, routine activity, and physiological factors.

Without this particulate nature of reality, it would be impossible to observe any phenomenon. This is more general characteristics that are common to all of the components of which it consists. Aggregates *do not* have characteristic patterns of survival. In fact, aggregates are deceiving because the observer does not distinguish its components. Such is the case with a nation's population or its workforce. If it does have a characteristic pattern of survival, it is termed a component. The concepts of "component" and "aggregate" need to be specifically defined when the theoretical perspective is applied to particular circumstances. Components and aggregates are defined by specific units of analysis. For example, the number of newborns in the month of August 1980 could be defined as an aggregate. The components might be perceived as the individuals born in that month, categorized by ethnic status and income status of the male parent. An economic example of an aggregate would be that of Gross Domestic Product (GDP) at any time (t) using a product approach. Components would be personal consumption expenditure, gross private domestic investment, government purchases of goods and services, and net exports all at time t. This treatise will elaborate the concepts of component and aggregate as they apply to human welfare from a longitudinal perspective.

Matter has been discovered to consist of molecules, atomic particles, and particles at a subatomic level. It is known that energy and matter are directly related ($E = mc^2$). There are numerous physical as well as ecological perspectives on the nature of matter and energy. The first law of thermodynamics is that of the conservation of energy, stating that mechanical energy can be changed into heat energy at a defined rate. The second law of thermodynamics states that heat cannot pass from a cold body to a warm body. Later, Planck developed quantum theory in his efforts to explain radiant energy. He found that radiation is not a continuous process but that energy is emitted in small packets of various sizes always containing an integral multiple of units called *quanta*. Matter and energy are thus, at their physical and energetic base, particulate in nature. Particle theory is constantly evolving and continues to depend on the construction of different forms of particle acceleration and equipment as well as changing theory. With this evolution of particle theory, the laws of conservation continue to be found to be true. Fermi's evolution of Pauli's theory of beta decay preserved the conservation laws governing the world of atomic and subatomic particles.

These physical perspectives have applicability to humans and related systems. First, it is important to understand that all human reality is "particulate" at its base. Particulate means that it appears in some unitary form or, if aggregate, a blend of unitary forms. These units may exist at one time, exist over time, cease to exist, or change. From a theoretical and applied perspective the major analytical decisions to etc.). It is clear; the detailing of observations about this one home could progress for some time before all possibilities are exhausted. A contractor would look at the home in terms of the cost of time and materials it took to build the home and his expected and real profit. An owner would be more concerned with the expenses of the house, the functional and aesthetic qualities of the home, its location and other factors. That the contractor and the home-owner have different perspectives is important. The contractor is concerned with every 2 x 4, door, piece of particle board, shingle, fixture, furnishing and cabinet used in the construction of the house as well as the labor (hours) and money (dollars and cents) invested in its construction. This truly reveals the particulate nature of the house as well as the contractor's concerns. The owner of the house has a specifically different set of "particulate" preferences and concerns. When aggregated, the materials and the concerns result in something called a "house". Similarly, from an owner's perspective, it becomes important because of the combination of particulate characteristics that the house has. The number of bedrooms, floor space, carpeting, furnishings, location, floor plan, and even the "feel" of the house are particulate in nature.

From the perspective of human perception, the particulate nature of reality becomes blurred. There is an illusion of wholeness. We do not see a light wave as a composite of photons (which it is). We do not see a house, as we live in it, as a combination of doors, windows, appliances, electrical wiring, paint, boards, etc. It is unnecessary for us to do so from a functional perspective. Nonetheless an underlying, particulate, reality is there. It is understood the particulate reality relevant to human growth and development, human behavior, and the behavior of systems they are part of that is essential to the formulation of effective policies at an individual and a macro level. The connections are present. It is important to recognize this in any theoretical perspective developed for any discipline of thought.

A similar case can be made for the composition and functioning of the human being. Human particulate nature is undeniable. The structure of amino acids and chemicals that constitute our cells, organs, systems and bodies are examples of how particulate reality is organized into components and aggregates, depending on the frame of reference. From the perspective of those who study humans, the diversity of perspectives is far-ranging. A molecular geneticist is trying to define the structure of a small segment of the human genome while a political scientist is involved in the study of the impact of sound bites or language on public voting patterns. A cell biologist is trying to assess the chemical functioning of mitochondria, while a population theorist is interested in defining multivariate explanations of rates of conception that of the component. Units distribute themselves in a pattern of survival that is a property of the component and its interaction with the external environment. Two or more components, in turn, make up an *aggregate*. An aggregate has one or more general characteristics which are common to all of the components of which it consists. Aggregates may have characteristic patterns of survival. In fact, aggregates are deceiving because the observer does not distinguish its components. Such is the case with a nation's population or its work force. The concepts of "component" and "aggregate" need to be specifically defined when the theoretical perspective is applied to particular circumstances. Components and aggregates are defined by specific units of analysis. For example, the number of newborns in the month of August, 1980 could be defined as an aggregate. The components might be perceived as the individuals, born in that month, categorized by ethnic status and income status of the female parent. An economic example of an aggregate would be that of Gross Domestic Product (GDP) at any time (t) using a product approach. Components would be personal consumption expenditure, gross private domestic investment, government purchases of goods and services, and net exports all at time t. This book will elaborate the concepts of component and aggregate as they apply to human welfare from a longitudinal perspective.

The following chapter addresses focusing one's attention.

CHAPTER 5

ATTENTION AND OBSERVATION

The last chapter concluded with an observation about particular forms of focusing one's attention. I will label this as *practices*. The general similarity among most practices is that they require focusing attention of the human mind and body. The range of practices that one can engage in varies from meditation and yoga to running and other various forms of physical exercise. There are two essential characteristics of a practice: initially, it is done with some regularity, and second, it allows the individual to focus his or her attention.

The initial character of practice—that it is done

with regularity—indicates that the practice occurs in a continuum of moments, none of which can be repeated exactly as it was done the preceding time. Furthermore, the repetition of the practice may add to a person's skills or adeptness at the practice. Third, focusing on the practice allows the individual to see and be with great clarity, not being distracted by irrelevant thoughts and having a purity of concentration.

When we wish to concentrate our efforts, attention and observation are sometimes blocked, blurred, or shaped by thoughts or memories of the past. Pleasant, neutral, or unpleasant memories are stored in altered form by the mind, the solar plexus, or the fascia-musculature system. All may store energy from these experiences. This stored energy, in the form of energized memories, has a life all its own and affects our daily behavior and skeletal alignment. Psychoanalysis makes an effort to access these energized memories and put them in context. In psychoanalysis, the patient free-associates to bring to consciousness buried memories and, with the assistance of a trained psychoanalyst, put them into an understanding that relieves some forms of stress in the patient's life.

There are also two forms of body therapy that are worthy of mentioning: Rolfing and body signal work. Rolfing (1989) is concerned with structural alignment. In Rolfing, a certified Rolfer assesses the body's alignment and applies deep pressure on the fascia and musculature to realign the body. Rolfing consists of a set of ten sessions. Pre- and post-Rolfing photographs are taken and compared to assess the changes that have been made.

Body signal work (Moore, 1990) consists of scanning the body in a relaxed state to locate areas of body tension and understand the source of that tension. Once the area of tension is found, the musculature is tensed, and the first words that come to mind are repeated. Physical actions to purge the muscle memory are undertaken, and repair work is done. During the repair work, the patient proceeds to love him- or herself as is.

There remain two parts of the body and its nervous system about which little is known—the solar plexus is located at the back of the body. This mass of interconnected nerves, because of its complexity, remains a difficult area to research. What memories and emotions does the solar plexus maintain? We can only depend on future research to unveil some of the solar plexus's mysteries. The second part of the nervous system that remains a mystery is the brain and spinal cord.

Despite this and other remaining questions about how we observe, participation in a practice improves our powers of observation. We can focus our attention and observation with an uncluttered mind in each moment in which we engage. By attending to and observing the continuity of life, our experience becomes richer and we become more aware. The uniqueness of this continuity of moments, by definition, offers newness to life.

How we use our powers of observation and augment them offers us a rich and diverse world. Humanity has created methods of observation that have contributed greatly to our abilities to see life at all levels of observation—particle accelerators, electron microscopes, chemical analysis, thermometers, gas chromatographs, biomolecular analysis, ocular microscopes of differing powers, mirrors, spectrometers, X-rays, magnetic resonance instruments, CT scans, visual observation, ocular telescopes, and radio and radar telescopes. These and more instruments and techniques help observe and sometimes record the now as it becomes the past.

Our eyes are but one of the many tools humans have for observing the future, present, and past moments. Our senses of smell, touch, hearing, and taste lend to the qualities of life we experience. We have developed scientific and mathematical techniques for telling what is correct and what is mistaken. Some scientific research can quantify expected error levels. But existence is not always predictable. The next chapter will focus on what occurs in the continuity of our observation.

CHAPTER 6

DECLINING, MAINTAINING, AND GROWING

The verbs *declining, maintaining,* and *growing* are used for this chapter title because they indicate process— in particular, the process in which all organic and inorganic life is engaged. Businesses and industries are all involved in one or more of these processes. Cities, states, nations, and individuals can all be characterized with these three terms, which are indicative of a continuing now. Although these moments are unlikely to be relived or exactly recaptured, we can understand something of their nature.

How are these three terms to be used in furthering our understanding of life as process? First, it is necessary to establish a convention that will be used throughout this chapter. Assuming that *process* means change, a symbol for the direction of change will prove useful. To that end, the following words and symbols of change and balance will be used:

>change in the direction of the arrowhead

<change in the direction of the arrowhead

Declining is deterioration in composition, strength, vigor, or character; deterioration. *Maintaining* equals a steady state or homeostasis; in economics a near equilibrium. *Growing* is becoming greater in quantity, size, extent, or intensity.

Thus, for our three terms used in the title, the following symbolizes their relationship:

<>deteriorating<>----maintaining<>----<>growing<>

The <> marks at the extremes of this symbolic relationship indicate that the extremes may proceed to a further extent than provided by the terms *deteriorating* and *growing*. If a house is burned down by a fire, it is demolished. Alternatively, a business or industry may continue to grow until it is merged with another business or industry and loses its distinct identity. This growth or decline may take place in any direction. Let's take a look at some other polar opposites.

<>hating<>----<>knowing<>----<>loving<>

Hating can deteriorate into violence; loving can escalate into dependency. Both are signs that a relationship has changed. The status of knowing someone is a steady-state or homeostatic situation.

A physical characterization of a person's state of nutrition could be characterized as follows:

<>starving<>----<>satisfied<>----<>satiated<>

Starving degenerates into kwashiorkor and death.

Satiation can result in obesity and death. Being satisfied represents a homeostatic or steady state.

A characterization of a person's mental state follows:

<>depressed<>----<>settled<>----<>manic<>

Depression can degenerate into loss of hope. Elation can elevate into manic behavior. The condition of being settled is one of being in a homeostatic or steady state.

The process of understanding the extremes of our behavior, our behavior in moderation, and what is detrimental to our being or the being of others provides useful understandings. One of the important aspects of doing this is recognizing that life is a process in which change is ever present. Secondly, we *may* have the ability to choose where we want to be along many of these spectra.

All reality, including space, is in process. All reality

consists of continua. The continuum at the basis of reality is this:

<>antimatter<>----<>matter<>----<>energy<>

Continua are a conceptual way of describing different aspects of our diverse physical, biological, social, economic, and behavioral worlds. Another way of conceptualizing all continua is as follows:

<>diminishing<>----<>maintaining----<>growing<>

This continuum purposely uses gerunds to indicate an ongoing process. Also, at the terminal stages of the continuum are arrowheads pointing beyond the concepts of diminishing and growing. Why? This is so because diminishing can continue to the point of diffusion or extinction. This is also true of the concept of growing. Growing can continue to the time of diffusion or extinction. This represents a definitional issue for the observer.

Continua can be multivariate as well as multidimensional despite being portrayed linearly. Only some continua are linear.

As components and aggregates of reality are observed in their general and specific forms, several descriptive truths will become evident. These truths fit into a systematic theoretical perspective that is useful in understanding many different types of phenomena. The focus of this treatise is on humans, their components, their context, and the relationships they are part of, participate in, and create. In these matters of focus, there is a general, relative continuum that can be characterized in the following way:

<>deficit<>----<>equilibrium<>----<>surplus<>

Application of this general continuum, in specific and diverse ways, is a major focus of this book.

CHAPTER 7

FROM IDEOLOGY TO IDEALISM

Everyone has a choice in life whether to believe in an ideology, be a pragmatist, or be an idealist. Such a choice may be a general one, be a specific ideology, or be made on a choice-by-choice basis. One may choose to be of a specific religion. If in effect one chooses a specific religion, he or she has chosen an ideology if the religion has certain tenets, beliefs, or guidelines for behavior that it expects followers to adhere to.

There are advantages and disadvantages to any position along this spectrum. Those who are ideologues run the risk of getting into situations in which they have beliefs that do not fit the context in which they find themselves. This causes the condition known as cognitive dissonance. People who are ideologues may live satisfactory lives among similarly believing individuals. When they are in situations with people who have different beliefs or are more outspoken, they become more retiring.

Pragmatists are individuals who adapt to the situation in which they are. Politicians can be pragmatic; however, they may adhere to a combination of any two or three of the belief systems. Pragmatists do better as politicians as they adapt better to the variety of issues they encounter. They can compromise and listen to the viewpoints of others. Pragmatists know there is more than one way to solve a problem—and that sometimes there is a best way. Pragmatists are more able to bring about compromise and reconciliation. Politicians are beholden to several pulls and pushes. For one, they are responsible to the constituents who elected them. As a second force, they are responsible to their own consciences. A third force in some political systems is the party to which the politicians belong. In authoritarian governments, the primary concern is about control.

Idealism is found among individuals who are dedicated to the tenets of one or more principles or outcomes. There are several types of idealism devoted to several types of ends and to certain belief systems. Idealists are individuals who are dedicated to a purpose or cause that is usually intended for the greater good.

The three sources of these general approaches to life are heavily influenced by factors such as family belief system, exposure to education, age, and wealth.

Ideologues, pragmatists, and idealists coexist in the everyday world. Their differences and similarities promote both harmony and discord in society. The ability to get past different and diverse characteristics is the principle ability of a society to remain peaceful. Early humans coexisted in tribes, and this coexistence meant that consolidation had to occur before tribes could dissolve. Much of humanity still remains in tribes, and differences among tribes persist as a major source of disagreements and prejudices.

CHAPTER 8

REASON AND FAITH

The meaning that will be applied to the word *reason* will be "to form conclusions, judgments, or inferences based on facts." A *fact* is a truth known by actual experience or observation, or something known to be true. It is within our human experience that two individuals observing the same object, happening, or incident can have different views about what they have seen. For this reason, the scientific method has been developed to verify facts and discover new ones. The scientific method consists of formulating a hypothesis, developing a method of experimentation, collecting data, analyzing the data, and drawing conclusions. In the scientific process, there is a final step that reaches but a small portion of the population. That process is the dissemination of information in an understandable form.

For this reason, society has a group of highly trained individuals who communicate among themselves in languages adapted to their unique disciplines. This mutual communication serves some important functions. Initially, it offers an opportunity to review work to be published to ensure that scientific protocol is observed. These scientists both criticize one another's work as well as communicate with one another about additional research or investigation that needs to be done. New ideas, theories, and experiments are developed to further human knowledge. It is this process of thinking and action that leads to new ideas in medicine, technology, military goods, consumer goods, product improvement, and activity in human life. In juxtaposition to the scientific method is action on the basis of faith. An appropriate example of this is our developing and almost unconscious belief in gravity. Repeated experience shows the young, developing child that if he or she cannot maintain his or her balance, a fall to the floor or ground will soon occur. Gravity is an unseen force, but its effects are not. Scientists have formulated an equation describing the force of gravity, but this formulation is not experienced by the child. The child learns about gravity from experience, not from a textbook.

Faith is used to explain existence within a belief system that may or may not include scientific reasoning. Lacking an explanation for certain natural phenomena, individuals may turn to faith. In fact, their faith may be used to explain the unexplainable. Faith may include scientific belief as well as a belief system based in science. When people find it worthwhile to celebrate their beliefs, a worship group, a congregation, or a church is formed. There may be established belief systems that extend culture-wide.

Most all peoples have a creation story. It's perplexing to try to imagine how this earth, its beauty, and its tragic moments have come to be formed. The eternal question arises, "How can something be formed out of nothing?" Despite the big bang theory, the question still remains. To answer this primary void in our experience, we often turn to faith.

The second set of questions that is universal to humanity is, "where do I go when I die? Is there life after death?" Cultures, churches, and civilizations have tried to provide answers to believers to whom these questions have occurred. In fact, some churches actively promote their solution to these questions as a way of molding human behavior in the present, whether it is by fear, reward, or understanding. The promise of punishment or salvation weighs importantly on the consciousness of many individuals.

The past and present of religious groups has been checkered. The building of the Egyptian pyramids, the Great Crusades, the Inquisitions, the Nordic warlords, the warring factions in Iraq and Afghanistan—all have been in search of domination or power. Beliefs and ideology have continued to keep the global political situation in flux. The average citizen and peasant are at the mercy of such forces and find themselves hiding from compelling or destructive forces.

What can faith do for the individual? As mentioned in an earlier chapter, it can provide a practice. Recognizing that there are powers outside oneself puts one's own existence in perspective. These powers are many times beyond one's control. This statement is not intended to bring on helplessness but to recognize a fact. One's practice can function as a source of personal calm and strength. If one's practice involves fellow believers, it may provide a social group that has magnified power due to its numbers, energy, and sense of purpose. In times of trial and suffering, the support provided by fellow believers can be an unsolicited grace.

How does one arrive at a centered existence in which there is clarity of mind and right action? I must admit that I do not have an answer to this question but encourage you to continue your search. There are multiple paths to finding a practice that is comfortable and settling to the individual. If you have not found such a practice, you are encouraged to do so.

CHAPTER 9

THE WORLD AS IT IS

This essay is not designed to advance any organizational agenda or ideal. It is not propagating any belief or ideology. It is not written from any particular ethnic or national view. It is written in the spirit of observing what life is, will possibly be, and has been (Krishnamurti, 1984). This essay and its contents call us to observe what has happened, is happening, and will be happening in the world. You are asked to think together with me but not necessarily be of the same mind. I have no authority to compel you to think as I do and would not want it if it were offered to me. So, come, let us observe together.

While each of us may be concerned with our own personal salvation, you and I must have a larger concern about what humanity is facing. We must put aside our ethnic, religious, and national labels. As human beings in this world, what are we to do? We watch the news stories concerning plagues of daily murder, bombings, kidnappings, and destruction. We may even pass over them due to our desensitization to them. If they happen to us, then we respond by asking for the protection of governmental health, law enforcement, or military authorities.

In the United States, the continuing and increasing poverty, the need for educational equity, the millions without health care protection, and a looming environmental crisis are accepted as part of the fabric of life. We sense that we are incapable of doing anything about it. This is factual; we are not dealing with what is actually occurring. This is urgent. It is important for us to be free of our ethnic, national, and in some cases religious ties. In the United States, individuals have become uninterested in much of what occurs on a daily basis. A hopeful sign was the recent statement of the American people in their vote for their senators and representatives. Yet even this is being ignored.

The world is populated by thought and speech. From architecture to newsprint, from transportation to magazines, and from our homes to TV sets, thought is required. Print media and television shows are humans' creation. As every book in the world is derived from human thought, no book is sacred. Many TV programs are fictional or consist of game shows conjured up to test the wits of contestants and viewers. We live in a world that is partially a shadow without substance.

We have to examine things very closely and understand the urgency of beginning to act in the ways available to us. To do this, we need to examine our human and collective consciousness. As an individual, you are beset by a range of thoughts and emotions. These include what you think and feel, your pleasures and fears, your loves and hatreds, your anxieties and certainties, elation and depression, joy and sorrow. As an individual, these are what make you human. An initial step, and perhaps the biggest one, is understanding these aspects of ourselves. Understanding right action is based on a clear comprehension of both our own and our collective consciousness. It is far easier to act from clarity than it is from confusion.

Our culture is highly materialistic. We are bound up, as the advertisement says, "in searching for the high life." Individuals and families are bound up in a persistent search for betterment of their material circumstances. What is enough is poorly defined in the minds of many individuals, and individuals become what they possess.

The larger picture is enough to put our concerns

into perspective. We live in a universe that itself is a wave form. The big bang was ignorant of time. The theory I advance is that there are black holes. The black holes merge until they become of such density and size that they explode into another universe. This takes trillions and trillions of light years. The universe does its thing without attention to our perspective on time.

CHAPTER 10

DISCOVERING ONESELF AND THE WORLD

I recognize the uniqueness of each individual and my inability to speak directly to each individual's circumstances. Each of us has a unique set of issues and methods of finding how to define ourselves. It is possible, however, to examine one's life and determine whether transformation is desired or possible. Some may be subject to the pressures and stresses of daily life. These pressures and stresses come from a variety of sources—financial, consumption, work, family, and the compulsion to conform or keep up with the Joneses. Time pressures and the stress of keeping a daily schedule are often with us.

But in this essay, I ask you to put these pressures and stresses aside. We are communicating as friends. We may bring to consciousness any of our past and current concerns about our well-being and that of others. Dedicating yourself to self-examination is a necessary part of the healing process for yourself and the larger human community.

Much of the world and many of the individuals in it are suffering. Unconscious fears, anxieties, insecurities, grief, and sorrows are found at the depths of the human unconscious. The price of not understanding this is more violence and confusion in the world. In addition, we are in the process of damaging the very planet we are living on. The earth's air, its animal inhabitants, and its flora are being put at risk. Look for yourself. What do you observe? Disappearing coral reefs, melting glaciers, a disappearing ozone layer, irregular weather patterns—all are part and parcel of environmental degradation. Human life is expendable, with violence occurring in Iraq, Afghanistan, Chad, the Sudan, Somalia, Syria, and other countries. Poverty is the dominant condition of part of the world's population. Observe and think. How can this be? A necessary step is to understand ourselves, our fears, our pain and suffering, our sadness, and our grief. If we do this as individuals, we not only have a voice but can also take action against the suffering, the violence, and the environmental degradation.

What is the likelihood of this happening? It doesn't look good. How can entire cultures whose leaders issue fear-based messages offer hopeful voices and actions in the face of world violence and hostilities? Examine these worldwide conditions for yourself. Are we the proverbial ostriches burying our heads in the sand?

We are like individuals on a train, eating in the dining car. Outside, the landscape passes by almost unnoticed as we concentrate on conversation, ordering, or the food. Yet we are not fully aware of something essential to our existence. We are in a relative relationship to all around us, including the landscape. We are in relationship to our family, our mates, the individuals we meet, the world community, and yes, the landscape. The landscape passes by and continues to exist. This is similar to much we experience. It has gone beyond the point where we can ignore that which is out of sight or out of the continuity of existence. Planet earth and its inhabitants know little of the impending consequences of our treatment of the planet. Soon it will be too late for certain ecosystems and areas that we have long taken for granted.

More than anything, this essay is a statement about life as process and its relativity to a larger context. What is needed is to change the consequences of that process. This process does not necessarily mean progress. That, in fact, depends on the choices we make. Our material technology needs to be used in a positive way to affect our environment. Let us be aware of life as process of individuals, families, communities, governments, and cultures. At what time will individuals take responsibility (the ability to respond) for their part in the process?

Do we have the will?

CHAPTER 11

APPLYING WHAT WE HAVE LEARNED

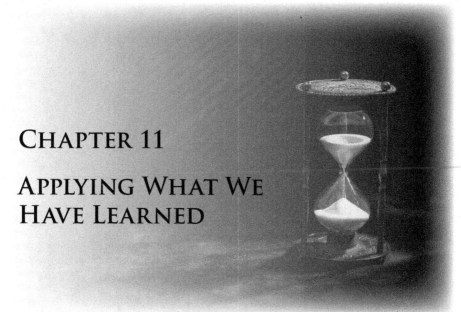

What is the point of this book? It is to apply the theoretical views presented to any population in the United States and the context.

The usefulness of the theoretical framework presented is found in its application to the situation of the individual in US society. The smallest unit of analysis in the United States is the individual. The individual exists in the context of an environment. The environment varies for each individual and in each circumstance. Let's define the context.

Environment refers to the air, water, living space, availability of medical care, availability of income and jobs.

REFERENCES

Csikszentmihalyi, Mihaly. *Flow*. New York: Harper & Row, 1990.

Krishnamurti, J. *The Flame of Attention*. Krishnamurti Foundation Trust Foundation Limited. New York: Harper & Row, 1984.

Likert, R. A. "A Technique for Measurement of Attitudes." *Archives of Psychology* 140, no. 55 (1932).

Moore, W. H. *Body Signals: What Is Your Body Trying to Tell You?* Washington, D.C. : Self-published. 1990.

Munshi, J. A. *Method of Constructing Likert Scales.* Accessed April 28, 2015 by title of article.

Murphy, G., and R. A. Likert. *Public Opinion and the Individual: A Psychological Study of Student Attitudes on Public Questions with a Retest Five Years Later.* Oxford, England: Harper Books, 1938.

Rolf, I. P. *Rolfing: Reestablishing the Natural Alignment and Structural Integration of the Human Body for Vitality and Well-Being.* Rochester, VT: Healing Arts Press, 1989.

Sandow, S. A., with C. Bamber and J. W. Rioux. *Durations: The Encyclopedia of How Long Things Take.* Avon, NY: Times Books, 1977.